The Jesus Equation

By James Alford

Righteousness Ministries c/o
Righteousness Publishing
P.O. BOX 782
Smyrna, GA 30081

For more Information goto:
www.thejesusequation.com
www.righteousnessministries.org

Copyright 2012 By James Alford
All Rights Reserved.

ISBN 978-0988764606

THE JESUS EQUATION

This book is dedicated to all those who love the truth.

Contents

Preface..6

1. Opening the Door...............................9

2. The Enemy's Game...........................19

3. The Left Hand of Fellowship.............27

4. The Spirit of Babel............................39

5. Dividing the Brethren........................51

6. Angel of Light....................................61

7. Name Above All Names....................79

Preface

"The kingdom of heaven is likened unto a man which sowed good seed in his field: But while men slept, his enemy came and sowed tares among the wheat, and went his way. But when the blade was sprung up, and brought forth fruit, then appeared the tares also. So the servants of the householder came and said unto him, Sir, didst not thou sow good seed in thy field? from whence then hath it tares? He said unto them, An enemy hath done this. The servants said unto him, Wilt thou then that we go and gather them up? But he said, Nay; lest while ye gather up the tares, ye root up also the wheat with them. Let both grow together until the harvest: and in the time of harvest I will say to the reapers, Gather ye together first the tares, and bind them in bundles to burn them: but gather the wheat into my barn" (Matthew 13:24-30).

In Matthew 13, the field is the world, the sower is Jesus Christ, the seed sown are the children of God, and the tares are the children of the devil.

THE JESUS EQUATION

The words Jesus spoke two thousand years ago are just as relevant today. The devil has constantly sought to plant and grow evil in our midsts from the start of time.

We should all be confident that Jesus Christ will return. When he returns he will be looking for a church "without spot or wrinkle." This church is not in any particular location and neither does it consist of any particular building. This church consists of all those in the world who love and follow Jesus Christ. When Jesus returns he will bless the holy with everlasting life and the unholy will receive eternal damnation.

Chapter 1

Opening the Door

"Behold, I stand at the door, and knock: if any man hear my voice, and open the door, I will come in to him, and will sup with him, and he with me" (Revelations 3:20).

I Almost Lost Him

As I sat looking across the vast crowd of people I felt an excitement rise up in me. There were all these cool people gathered for the sake of what I thought was a hidden truth. We were waiting for this man to speak who had caught the attention of so called "enlightened youth" across the United States

THE JESUS EQUATION

and abroad. He was referenced in many rap songs and had written hundreds of little books on religion. He had even written a book that looked identical to the Bible and it was call the holy tablets. After reading the first page of this book you knew it was no Holy Bible, it was completely different. Being a young man searching for truth, I felt as if I had found the light. As the man rose to speak the crowd rose in excitement. His message at first seemed engaging, but then something happened. He looked across the crowd and it appeared as if he was looking directly at me and he started to curse the name of Jesus. Every time he cursed the name of Jesus it was as if he was striking me with a whip. As he continued saying those words, my eyes began to fill with tears. The words he used for Jesus were horrible and a great offense to me. These feelings seem to have come out of nowhere, since I had stopped believing in the word of God a while before this event. That one moment drew me back to Christ. I started researching the things this man had written and discovered many lies and deceit within the texts. I found that he was basically giving people lie sandwiches....throw a few truths on the outside and they will bite right in. When you bite into a lie sandwich you only find out it's a lie when you bite into it and if you are too hungry you probably won't even notice.

    As I thought about how I got mixed up with this cult, I remembered the years prior and the desire I had for Jesus. Even as a very young child my heart reached out to him and he reached for back for me. One night Jesus had come to me in a dream and told me it was time to go. I asked him for some more time and he told me he would give me a day. I spent the next day praying and getting my heart right so that I would go to heaven. The next night I was ready but he allowed me to stay. From this point I found myself constantly asking questions about Jesus and faith. My mind was immature but I knew that there was something in Jesus that I needed. When some ministers would preach, I would feel a desire for Jesus. I prayed to him nightly with hopes and desires, fears and frustrations. There was something about the name of Jesus that pulled on me, something that would not let me go. As I got older I felt the desire for spiritual power. I wanted it through God but I was confused with what it meant to have power from God. I started to attempt to try to read minds through ESP, I tried to move objects with my mind, and I considered various magical items. I had an intense desire for power that I wanted to satisfy. I read books and listened to tapes, looking to tap into power. I even ordered a book off a television commercial called "power for living". I would also try to read the bible but it was always very confusing to me. This frustration in the bible, lead me to other works that were easy to embrace.

     As I got into my late teens, I started to follow the teachings of that cult because I had lost my zeal for Jesus. I stopped believing in the Bible, but I still believed in supernatural power. One night, while some friends were over we started playing the Ouija board. We asked this board all types of questions and it seemed to be speaking back. It would lie and then tease and served as some scary entertainment. After I had played with this board, it was as if I had entered a different life. All hell broke loose.....My new car

THE JESUS EQUATION

transmission blew up, later my car engine blew up, someone broke in my car while it was being serviced, someone stole my dogs, I got arrested twice in a few weeks, my power went out in my apartment and I couldn't get it turned back on, and I lost my longtime girlfriend. I consulted a few witches and one told me that I had been cursed and I spoke to another and she said that she could fix things and get my girlfriend back. I spoke with this witch daily and sent her money as requested. One day when I was returning home from work I saw a figure in rags walking in my neighborhood. I thought it might be a homeless person but it was odd in that I was so far from the downtown area. As I parked I looked closely at the figure and it had no head, no arms, and no legs. It was sliding across the ground towards me. I Immediately ran to my apartment and when I looked out the window it was gone. From that day on, I completely washed my hands clean of dabbling in witchcraft.

    Now, as a minister of the Gospel of Jesus Christ I realize that while I went through all these belief systems and occult powers as a youth, I had no idea the attack that was being laid out before me. Satan knew my zeal for Jesus as a young child and he went in for the attack before I ever recognized an attack was taking place. I thank God that he gave me grace in that season that my eyes could now see the deception in the world today. There was a plot designed just for me to remove Jesus out of my life.

    Sometimes God allows us to endure attacks and deception that we may learn from it. If you join the military you have to go to boot camp, and then you go into specialized training based upon your gifts and needs of the military at the time. We understand

THE JESUS EQUATION

by scripture that when we become Christians in this earthly realm, we sign up as soldiers in the Army of the Lord. Just as natural armies prepare their men to fight, so also God prepares his soldiers. This is the reason why Satan intensifies the fight against you when you grow in God. *"But call to remembrance the former days, in which, after ye were illuminated, ye endured a great fight of afflictions; Partly, whilst ye were made a gazingstock both by reproaches and afflictions; and partly, whilst ye became companions of them that were so used"* (Hebrews 10:32-33).

    The stronger you become in Jesus, the more you are able to put the devil under your feet. The devil knows that as Christian all of our authority rests with Jesus. If he can get us to put down Jesus or dilute our faith in him then we have nothing to fight with and are taken captive at the enemy's will. There is a war going on in the spirit world. A battle for souls in the spirit realm wages every day but most only see through their natural senses. I have come to understand that the spirit realm is more real than this natural existence that we live in. Satan would have us to try to rationalize, live, and figure things out according to the rules of this world, because when we dare to put our faith in Jesus, a doorway to the spirit opens and we as believers are able to dominate in the natural and the spirit.

    Satan desires to remove the "Jesus Equation" out of our lives. The definition of "equation" is the act of equating or making equal. Our belief in Jesus gives us access to his power and eternal life. The power of his name is the key to all. So we can say that Jesus = power , Jesus = eternal salvation, and Jesus = God. When we look in scripture Jesus says, *"I am the door:*

THE JESUS EQUATION

by me if any man enter in he shall be saved, and shall go in and out, and find pasture" (John 10:9). Jesus also said in, *"I and my father are one"* (John 10:30). Just looking at these two scriptures we see why Satan desires to remove Jesus. Jesus is the door to all the blessings of God.

Who Is Jesus

From the time Jesus was born the enemy sought to destroy him. He is the savior that mankind needed. We see in scripture that Jesus is referred to as the last Adam because he finished what was started with the first Adam. The first Adam allowed Satan to tempt him into eating the forbidden fruit and opened a doorway for the curse of sin to fall on mankind. Jesus through his sinless life and sacrificial death and resurrection destroyed the work that the devil had begun. Jesus is the key to separate us from the curse of sin. If you don't have Jesus then you are in captivity to sin and death. If you have Jesus, just as he overcame sin and death you also will overcome. For man's soul which was created through Adam to achieve everlasting life, the spirit of God attached to the womb of a woman and formed Jesus in the flesh. He is the combination of soul and spirit. Man being born with a soul when we received Jesus we access the spirit. Our relationship with Jesus ties us in to him and we become soul and spirit also. This is why it is written that Jesus is the first of many brethren. *"For whom he did foreknow, he also did predestinate to be conformed to the image of his Son, that he might be the firstborn among many brethren"* (Romans 8:29).

THE JESUS EQUATION

    In the book of Revelation it says that Jesus was slain since the beginning of time. He was prepared for us from the start even before Adam fell into sin. This is the power of Jesus. Often times we tie what's possible to natural laws. God is not tied to natural laws and its "his will be done" from start to finish. We must understand that the spirit realm is eternal, which means that it isn't tied to time. Everything that happens in the natural has already happened in the spirit. God our creator is a spirit and we worship him in spirit and in truth.
    Satan has since the beginning tried to separate man from God. It all started in the Garden of Eden... This was the place of God's first human creation and he said it was good. The devil was so angered over his eviction from heaven and his destination with damnation that he decided to wage war on Gods people. The plan seemed to be masterful in the beginning, Adam and eve disobey God and sin entered the world. Satan knows that God hates sin, so he unleashes the one thing God hates on his creation. From the early times until now, man's heart has grown more and more evil. Satan has been an active participant in turning man's heart away from God. In Genesis 6, we see that the sons of God made wives of the daughters of men. These sons of God are understood to be the angels that fell with Satan. So fallen angels took human wives and the bible says that the offspring became giants. We read even from the early times in scripture men looked to elevate themselves as gods. Nimrod and the tower of Babel served as the one of the early attempts to challenge God. From there false gods were worshipped regularly. Since the beginning, in every culture

THE JESUS EQUATION

across the planet, we see false gods elevated to the place of worship. Even God's own chosen people, "Israel" worshiped false gods even after God had delivered them out of the hands of slavery. Today, the differences in religions and beliefs are as different as the faces of men. This world has become melting pot of beliefs. Even in Christianity there are a few thousand different denominations, with their own set of beliefs, traditions, and rituals. Many have become frustrated with Christianity as a whole and are starting to turn to a universal type of belief in God. Many have lost the desire to love God and have resorted to just loving themselves. Jesus for many has been regulated to a symbol rather than a force to be reckoned with. It has been thousands of years since sin has been unleashed into the world and every day we see evil running rampart and there is no apparent hope for mankind. The one hope is the child of promise, Jesus, and through his victory on the earth he took the keys of sin and death from Satan and now sits on the right hand of God. There is no access to God or heaven except going through Jesus Christ.

"Verily, verily, I say unto you, He that entereth not by the door into the sheepfold, but climbeth up some other way, the same is a thief and a robber" (John 10:1).

To try to access God through other religions or other ways that are outside of Jesus is wrong and the devil knows it. This is why he tries to get people to worship other gods and tries to lead Christians into a false worship and a counterfeit relationship. Satan tells you sin is OK, God will take you as you are and you don't have to change, there are many ways to God, etc, etc, etc. If you don't know the game, Satan will even use Bible scripture to get you to see things his way instead of God's way. This was even attempted on Jesus himself. When Jesus first entered ministry he was driven into the wilderness to fast and pray by the Holy Spirit. While he was on his journey the devil took the opportunity to tempt him three times. On the second temptation the devil quoted scripture saying, *"for it is written, He shall give his angels charge concerning thee: and in their hands they shall bear thee up, lest at any time thou dash thy foot against a stone."* But Jesus resisted a counterfeit word from the devil and replied with another scripture.

     Jesus came and he overcame the world and oh how angry the devil is. Jesus came and made him his footstool and all that truly love and worship Jesus will make the devil their footstool also.

Chapter 2
The Enemy's Game

"*And the Lord said, Simon, Simon, behold, Satan hath desired to have you, that he may sift you as wheat:*" (Luke 22:31).

"*Lest Satan should get an advantage of us: for we are not ignorant of his devices*" (2 Corinthians 2:11).

<u>From The Beginning</u>

From the day you were born there has been a war on for your soul. Good and evil are set. Heaven and Hell are set. God and the devil are set. Your soul is the only movable piece and it is up to you which way you will move. Jesus and his word have been made available to you. Satan and his many paths have been made available to you. God would love for you to choose the pathway of righteousness. Satan wants you to choose anything else. This is the key for understanding Satan's game. Anything except Jesus is the goal! Anything can be another religion, lifestyle, or doctrine of devils. Anywhere Jesus is absent, Satan is at work. Satan thought that getting mankind to commit a sin was sufficient to cut them off from God, but through grace God allowed for Jesus to be our bridge to him. This bridge is our only lifeline to God through our faith in Jesus. Since we are able to come out of sin and be received into everlasting life Satan has to cut off our source. This is to eliminate a need, desire, love, obedience, to Jesus.

    Through my research and spiritual revelation I have determined that Satan likes to attack our relationship with Jesus from three separate angles. They are:

1. Lifestyle
2. Thoughts
3. False Religion / Doctrine of devils

    When we think about sin we have to realize Satan is the master sinner. He fell from heaven for trying to exalt himself above God. He brought a third of heaven with him. He is the purest of evil and is a master at getting others to sin. Can you imagine something that is cunning enough to talk angels out of their place with God? He has used his skill from day one to lead men into sinful lifestyles. Gods answer for sin is Jesus.

The Problem with Sin

    If you want to separate yourself from God, have a sinful lifestyle. I remember a time I was discussing the Bible with a gentleman and a young lady walked up to me and asked, "What's the big deal with sin." I immediately said, "Everything! Jesus came because of sin. He died because of sin." She started to tell me how her mother used to preach to her, but she didn't see the big deal as long as she wasn't hurting anyone. This is the mindset of many that refuse to live a life pleasing to God have. It's hard to see the suffering caused by sin, because the majority of it comes on judgment day. Satan works on the absence of judgment to convince people that hell and eternal damnation doesn't exist or won't affect them because God will understand that they were just living their life not bothering anyone. Some might ask, "What is sin?" and I always respond, "Anything outside the will of God.

Does living in sin make you evil?

"Little children, let no man deceive you: he that doeth righteousness is righteous, even as he is righteous. He that committeth sin is of the devil; for the devil sinneth from the beginning. For this purpose the Son of God was manifested, that he might destroy the works of the devil" (1 John 3:7-8).

Our lifestyles either tie us directly to God or directly to the devil. You cannot live in sin and claim to be with God. This biggest trick played on those who profess to be Christians with their lips but their lives are far from it. To be a child of God your actions need to line up with your words. Jesus said those that love him will do his commands.

Before I committed myself to Jesus Christ, I constantly lived a sinful lifestyle. My conversation was full of evil words, I listened to music that was unholy, and slept around with different women. Though I did all these things I was not evil in men's eyes and many asked me why I was so pressed to get saved. I had realized that I was a dead man walking. God is very serious about our lifestyles. In first Peter it says, "Be holy, for I am holy". "Holy", according to the original language the Bible was written means... blameless. God desires that we be blameless. It's hard to be blameless when we make all these lifestyle choices that tie us daily to unholy things. For instance, if a man and woman move in together without being married, they enter into a unholy union which is completely sinful to God. Even if the two people love each other and do good things for others, they have in God's eyes given their life over to sin. *"Flee fornication. Every sin that a man doeth is without the body; but he that committeth fornication sinneth against his own body"* (1 Corinthians 6:18).

    Marriage is honorable in all, the bed undefiled. God gave us an out for our sexual desires. All we have to do is chose a mate and marry them and then we can indulge in those pleasures. Satan has attacked marriages viciously. Christian divorce rates rival rates in non-Christians marriages. Satan knows that God has provided marriage as a way to avoid sin and live victoriously in Jesus Christ. The devil has a lot of experience attacking marriages. From the start he attacked Adam and Eve and convinced them to eat the forbidden fruit bringing death to the world.

    Satan has dressed sin up to be normal in life. Things that were only spoken of in shame are now out in the open. Sodom and Gomorrah fell to this deception. The sin in these cities reached up to

Heaven. God didn't say, "I know they are sinning, but they are just being themselves." He reigned fire and brimstone from heaven and destroyed all those who where dwelling there. God is just as real and powerful as he was thousands of years ago. The only difference is that now we have an advocate. His name is Jesus. He is holding back judgment until the end. The just will get everlasting life and the sinful will receive eternal damnation. *"So shall it be at the end of the world: the angels shall come forth, and sever the wicked from among the just, And shall cast them into the furnace of fire: there shall be wailing and gnashing of teeth"* (Matthew 13:49-50).

    I would suggest anyone who is riding the fence with God to fully embrace righteousness. It would be a shame to know the truth and still miss going to heaven. How many times have we heard of hypocrites in the church? Saying one thing and can barely get out of church service before they are doing evil. Satan wants a fleshly or sensual experience in church....an experience that will create a counterfeit relationship with God. Us being stubborn for sin, yet insisting we maintain a relationship with God without the need for change, creates a counterfeit relationship with the lord.

    At one of my first church services the musician we had hired made a pass at my wife after service. I couldn't believe it. How could someone play behind me preaching and then think to say something to my wife. People are active in church, but absent from the spirit of God. They say "I love Jesus", but many don't really know who Jesus is. Not really knowing who Jesus is allows doctrines of devils to rise up and confuse our relationship with God and also it allows

THE JESUS EQUATION

false religions to reign.

Divide and Conquer

Satan often uses a divide and conquer strategy to attack Christians and the church. Through offense and small twists in doctrine, ministries break up and form new churches. This scenario happens when someone reads a single scripture and says "they are not following that scripture in this church, and it is something that has to be followed." Offense then rises up and the people leave and start a church that emphasizes that scripture. I've seen it time and time again, I go to a church and they repeatedly mention that one piece of scripture over and over again in their services. Now there is nothing wrong with separating if the former church was really operating in error, but most of the division comes over small shifts in doctrine, and the new church hangs its hat on it and this small shift in forms the basis for the church's beliefs.

When I first started my ministry, I had a gentleman and his wife to come and help us get it going. They said that they had an organization that focused on bringing the church together and assisted small ministries to get started. I had spoken with him in the beginning about the church he came from and he told me that he had attended a seven-day Adventist church. He assured me that it was all about Jesus and he wasn't worried about minor differences in doctrine. He and his wife came regularly to services and were very active. I noticed during that time we also had people to show up desiring to help with the music also. They initially seemed as gifts from God, but this supposed gift quickly turned into a curse. One Sunday I had just wrapped up my sermon and the gentleman jumped up out of his seat and he said to me in a very angry tone, "WHO IN HERE IS WORKING ON SATURDAY, THEY NEED TO STOP IMMEDIATELY!!!" Seeing a spirit rise up in him, I quickly ushered him to the back to speak to him. He told me that "it was time to start having services on Saturday, because Saturday is the Sabbath." It was amazing to me because I had never seen this side of him. For a few months he had come and quietly participated and never caused any trouble.

    The Seventh Day Adventist whole doctrine is hung on having church service on Saturdays. If you ever listen to any of them speak, everything is tied to having the revelation of Saturday being God's holy day for Christians. I see it as a small twist in doctrine because I believe Christians are to make everyday a holy day for God. Seventh Day Adventists believe not having service on Saturday ties you to the devil. 17 million plus Christians worldwide separated from other protestant churches because of the belief that Saturday is the day to worship.

    Once Satan has all these divisions within the natural church, he sets in motion his next attack. It is to introduce doctrines into the church that completely destroy a Christian's relationship with Jesus. If the church were one under the headship of Christ, it would be extremely difficult to inject complete error, but since so many churches are at odds and so many divisions continue to happen it has become very easy for error to set in. So now we see self proclaiming Christian churches embrace homosexuality (sins of flesh), universalism (multi-faiths), and materialism.

THE JESUS EQUATION

Chapter 3
The Left Hand of Fellowship

"How art thou fallen from heaven, O Lucifer, son of the morning! how art thou cut down to the ground, which didst weaken the nations! For thou hast said in thine heart, I will ascend into heaven, I will exalt my throne above the stars of God: I will sit also upon the mount of the congregation, in the sides of the north: I will ascend above the heights of the clouds; I will be like the most High. Yet thou shalt be brought down to hell, to the sides of the pit" (Isa 14:12-15).

Satanism

After a few years of being saved I had started to look for ways to preach the gospel. The church I was attending at the time was too big for me to get an opportunity to speak and the easiest way for me to impact lives was to preach on the internet. I started to go into various chat rooms and began to profess the message of Jesus. My first stop was the Christian chat room and I found a whole bunch of people arguing about doctrine and other things. My second stop was the chat room for satanism and witchcraft. I thought this was a great opportunity to save a soul or two. I started to post messages about the gospel and at first my comments were being ignored and some would tell me to go back to the Christian room.

    After a few more posts a man instant messaged me and told me he wanted to talk more about Jesus. He told me that the story of Jesus Christ was near and dear to his heart, but that he had left Christianity because he felt that the Bible was very inaccurate and was not a true representation of God. I leaped on the opportunity to tell him about my journey and how I had left the faith for a season also. I then assured him that Jesus was the only way and I had come back from darkness also. At this point in the conversation is when things became very dark. He told me that he now worshipped the actual "good guy" of the Bible and his name was Satan. Instead of accepting the right hand of fellowship as we do in Christian churches, he was clear that he had accepted, "the left hand of fellowship". *The "Right" signifies Jesus as scripture states that he sits on the right hand of God.* The man I was chatting with on the internet insisted that the Christian God was the bad God and that's why he changed his faith. He thought that Adam and Eve should not have been punished for eating from the tree of the knowledge of good and evil and that Satan was just trying to help them to see the light. This man I was speaking to had completely sold himself out to Satan. It was interesting the amount of study he had done on the Bible and how he acknowledged God, yet he rejected him to face eternal damnation with Satan. He was completely turned from God's glory. This type of individual is different from most that are absent of Jesus in that he willing is accepting Satan as his god. He knows that the rejection of Jesus is cutting him off, yet in rebellion he stands.

      Satanism is the type of evil that caused a third of the angels in heaven to fall. It tries to paint evil as good and good as evil. Followers see Satan as someone who just wants you to have fun and enjoy your life. The founder of the Church of Satan is often quoted saying, "Do as thou wilt", which is in reference to how the devil desires that we all live in the flesh and enjoy all that we desire. There is the promise of blessings with curses following. When the angels fell there was no hope of salvation. All for the sake of deceptive words by Satan. He brought down a portion of heaven and then sought to destroy mankind with the same trick of rebellion against God. "Eat of the tree" "you will be like God", is what he said but immediately the curse of sin fell upon all mankind. He used this same tactic once again against Jesus, but Jesus resisted and overcame. So, now there is one standing between Satan's devices and humankind. He is the eternal high priest, Jesus Christ.

Occult

    Although Satanism is direct devotion to the evil one, others in the occult look to avoid this acknowledgement of evil and say they are justified in God's eyes. Many witches think they are good witches and that they fight evil. They communicate with the dead and command forces through spiritual means. They group spirits according to good and evil, not realizing that all things outside of God Jehovah are evil. They are tricked into believing that what they do helps, while all along they are bringing hell on earth. The devil loves this deception because he can get people to access evil directly and do his work without them knowing. The delusion is brought on those that practice the occult so that they won't turn away because of darkness. Satan knows that if he can keep these individuals practicing these black arts, when they die he can take them straight to hell. He doesn't want them to know that Jesus is the light and there is no access to God or power except through Jesus Christ. When we do a brief study of what God thinks about the occult we see...... *"When thou art come into the land which the LORD thy God giveth thee, thou shalt not learn to do after the abominations of those nations. There shall not be found among you any one that maketh his son or his daughter to pass through the fire, or that useth divination, or an observer of times, or an enchanter, or a witch, Or a charmer, or a consulter with familiar spirits, or a wizard, or a necromancer. For all that do these things are an abomination unto the LORD: and because of these abominations the LORD thy God doth drive them out from before thee"* (Deuteronomy 18:9-12).

    When God calls something an abomination, he is saying that it is disgusting to him. So to operate in any occult activity is disgusting to God. Accessing these powers is satanic power. God wants you to operate in his Holy Spirit power. When you embrace these things whether you know or not, you are on the side of the devil and Jesus is far from you.

I have heard many times wiccans say that they believe in Jesus. They do not realize that even devils believe. *"Thou believest that there is one God; thou doest well: the devils also believe, and tremble"* (James 2:19). To be a true follower of Christ is not just through our mouth, but through our actions also. If you receive Christ as your lord and savior, then you will not operate in witchcraft. This might seem to be simple, but Satan continues to convince people they can hang on to Jesus or acknowledge him as a spiritual master, and that they will be ok. He doesn't want them to know those that really accept Jesus will do his commands. The devil knows that all that work in the occult have their souls are tied to hell and a time has been appointed when judgement will fall. It is a grand deception for all that have desired power and have fallen for the cheap magical gifts of Satan.

Witchcraft is not to be played with. When a person operates in or is under the oppression of witchcraft, death is close by. Many years ago I was working in my yard and a man ran over to me and said that there was a dead man who had committed suicide in the house across the street. As we went to investigate we saw him hanging in the basement. It was determined that he was the landlord's son who had gone to the house to clean up after some tenants had left. In the room where he had killed himself, there was a witchcraft alter with demonic drawings. When I think about the previous tenants I realized that a lot of odd things were going on while they were there. Some other strange deaths had happened nearby. One day I had walked outside and was shocked to find my yard full of black crows. These birds had blacked out my property and didn't touch anyone else's property. I didn't understand at the time, but there was heavy demonic activity in the area because of the witchcraft that was coming out of that house.

In Hosea 4:6, God said that his people were destroyed because they rejected knowledge. I can't count the number of times I have seen Christians making decisions based on their daily horoscope and receiving or rejecting people based upon their zodiac sign. I have seen committed Christians integrate Yoga into their daily lives and refuse to let it go no matter what anyone said. Yoga is demonic to its root, yet the need to simplify things causes people to overlook it. Life at many times becomes very hectic and busy and people many times don't investigate things before they embrace them. Without spiritual knowledge the devil can bring much havoc and devastation to our lives.

Today the symbols of witchcraft and the occult are all around us. They range from the pentagram, to the all seeing eye, to pyramids. Pentagrams are used by witches as a symbol of magic and connection to Gaia or Mother Earth. They are used in rituals to conjure up devils and to give them directions. Any wearing of the pentagram should make Christians leery because of the nature of the symbol. Some will say that an upward pointing star represents white magic and a downward pointing start represents black magic. No matter how you spin it, pentagrams are evil.

The "all seeing eye" is another symbol we see a

lot of in society. It is so prevalent that it can be found on the back of the US dollar bill. Its origins are from the Egyptian sun god, Horus. Witches use this symbol to ward off evil spirits if that makes any sense. This symbol is extremely prevalent in the secular music industry. A whole book within itself can be written on the use of this symbol. Those who have magnified the "all seeing eye" in the music industry reads like the who's who of secular music. It makes obvious the power behind the scenes.

    I always say knowledge is good, but application is better. The realm of satanism, witchcraft, and the demonic is a place where most Christians do not want to venture. It is a place of fear and uncertainty in many committed Christians minds. This uneasiness is what the devil counts on and the reason why the works of these entities continue unchecked. Witchcraft is set to destroy the Church from the inside out. It serves to eliminate the work of Jesus Christ from our lives. The reason why it is so unchecked is because the knowledge of the workings of witchcraft are absent. Unlearned Christians look for a pointed hat, a broom stick, and a toad....All while the sweet lady that is readily active in the Church is cursing them everyday. Some might say that it is not that serious, but IT IS REALLY THAT SERIOUS.

    When Paul the Apostle was out preaching, a woman came to him and started declaring he was a great man of God and that everybody should listen to him. Paul, discerning the spirit that was operating in her, casted the spirit of divination out of her. Most people in ministry would embrace someone who came up and started exalting them and their ministry. The devil will exalt you, bring people to your church, make your name great among men, and bring you money and resources all in an effort to deceive. The enemy works for an end result and that is the spiritual death of you and everything around you. This manipulation is a form of witchcraft that Satan uses to penetrate and negatively affect the Church. The Bible says to be sober and vigilant because the devil is like a roaring lion walking around seeking who he may devour. Being sober means to not be in a place where you are not paying attention. Sometimes we go places and because of the perceived comfort of the location we let our guard down. We view the church building as a place of rest and we tend to let our guard down, when it is certain that many spiritually sick people are in the church. This is why God's ministers must be extra prayerful. We want the members and attendees, we want the volunteers, but we have to be able to discern the wheat from the tares. Jesus spoke of this when he gave a parable in ," Mat 13:30 Let both grow together until the harvest: and in the time of harvest I will say to the reapers, Gather ye together first the tares, and bind them in bundles to burn them: but gather the wheat into my barn."

    All while God is looking to sow righteousness in the church, the enemy is trying to plant tares among the wheat. God is allowing this to happen in this season, but in the end, the wheat will be separated and the tares destroyed.

Atheism

    While I attended school as a child, I took many science classes. The teachers talked about how the world was formed and how microbes evolved into water dwelling animals and how these animals learned to walk on dry land and how these walking animals soon started to think and speak and how we are now decendants of these ancient species. I always thought it ws strange that we never learned the version of events from the Bible...but to go on to the next grade I had to pass these classes and agree with the text. We studied the big bang theory and the other theories about how the world got here and how the earth and the universe are billions of years old. The one thing that stood out to me was that there were various opinions on these subjects from various scientists and no one could ever come to an absolute on anything. These scientists are elevated as great men of understanding and wisdom. Some scientists are so beloved that people will gather by the thousands and sit at their feet to hear the wisdom they have to share.

    One might say that evolution is a religion itself because it is based hugely upon belief (theory) also. Most don't understand that science is full of theory and hypothesis and has many gaping holes to it and many things understood are tied to just believing. Yet religion is frowned upon in school because it is tied to belief. I realize now that this indoctrination in school challenges childhood thinking and proceeds to into adulthood. Children's minds are formed when they are small. Their way of thinking and how they piece the world together is formed at an early age. Children get spirit-filled teaching for 1 hour per week and worldly teaching for 40 hours. Now we wonder why the younger generation is growing up with a resistant mind on God and religion. It seems as with each

THE JESUS EQUATION

younger generation, the commitment to God becomes more and more diluted. This dilution has resulted in many youth rejecting God all together.

The rejection of God in the schools I believe has led to disasterous results in our families and in society. We all remember Columbine High School and how the armed teenagers attacked the school and shot and killed many. The one story in particular with this event has always stayed with me is when the gunman walked into the classroom and asked the professing Christians to stand up. Only one person stood up. She was shot dead on the spot.

It's now more than ever that atheism has a voice that is growing and challenging everything in relation to God. It started many years ago with prayer at football games, then with prayer in schools, and it continues to rare its ugly head seeking to silence everything in relation to God. I recently saw on the news that a man asked for someone to say the blessing for food at a meeting and he is now in criminal trouble.

A bank was recently raided by the FBI because the Federal Reserve didn't like that they had Bible verses on their website and that they wore Christian jewelry at the office. They were ordered to remove anything that was resembled Jesus or Christianity. After much resistance and attention was brought to this situation, they were allowed to continue as usual. The homosexual lifestyle is now taught in some schools and other children are taught that it is okay. This goes directly against Christian teachings but is presented to many of our children as the something that is normal.

Our Christian beliefs stay under attack in the schools. The enemy wants to intimidate us into giving up on Jesus. He doesn't want us to openly profess our faith and he wants us to lose faith in God's power. Anything but Jesus Christ is the goal, because anything but Jesus leads to destruction. There is a reason that Jesus said in Matthew 7:13-14, "Enter ye in at the strait gate: for wide *is* the gate, and broad *is* the way, that leadeth to destruction, and many there be which go in thereat: Because strait *is* the gate, and narrow *is* the way, which leadeth unto life, and few there be that find it." With all the choices on the shelf, many will find it hard to believe that Jesus is the only thing that can save them. With so many choices, many ways to destruction follows.

Satan doesn't care what you worship or if you don't worship anything at all he just wants to get Jesus out of your life. The strategy of the devil is to throw everything up against the wall. He starts false religions, injects error into Christian faith, and works to destroy the Christian faith all together on the back end. When I used to work in sales distribution our strategy was to shove as many products on the shelves as the distributors would take and then we would through various sales tactics convince customers to take all the product off the shelf. We would do this process over and over again facilitating a free flow of our product. This is how Satan works. He puts every type of false religion, every false doctrine, every work of the flesh, ever level of carnal understanding and puts it on the shelf. Then he leads you down the row and offers you a selection of everything on the shelf.

When I go to the grocery store, many times I don't have an idea of what I want, it takes me a lot longer to choose because the selection is so vast. Many times I would end up asking someone nearby "what's good" or I would just grab something because I was tired of searching. The devil plays off our weary ways in wanting to just settle on something. He will send along someone who will give you advice on one religion or another and people will pick religion off the advice of peers or their environment.

    I certainly believe that if Christianity was oppressed in America you would see the number of self professing Christians decrease by huge numbers. Atheists tend to reject Christianity and all things religious because they become confused or frustrated will all the things on the shelf. They are trying to make sense of everything and nothing seems to add up from their understanding, so they reject everything. If you are convinced into selecting something on the religion shelf, Satan will carry you into confusion and cause you to dismiss everything, especially Jesus Christ.

Chapter 4
The Spirit of Babel

<u>The God Complex</u>

      Each time God does a work, evil works its way into the work. From Adam and Eve, to Noah, to the Nation of Israel, time and time again God refreshed and started with a new people and the end result continued to be bad. In the Genesis period of biblical history, Noah's family was chosen from among the earth's population to repopulate the earth. God was saddened by what the world had become *"And GOD saw that the wickedness of man was great in the earth, and that every imagination of the thoughts of his heart was only evil continually"* (Genesis 6:5). This wickedness of man had come about just like in the garden, by the work of Satan. The Bible says, *"There were giants in the earth in those days; and also after that, when the sons of God came in unto the daughters of men, and they bare children to them, the same became mighty men which were of old, men of renown"* (Genesis 6:4). Satan's band of fallen angels came to earth and cohabitated with the women and produced hybrid offspring. These offspring became giants and ruled the land. God had to purge the world of this evil and so he allowed the flood to engulf the earth. Noah and his family were the only ones to survive this flood and so through his family the world was repopulated. Of course as the generations rose up they became more and more evil and they desired to reach God. As they organized among themselves, they built a tower in an effort to reach God. *"And the whole earth was of one language, and of one speech. And it came to pass, as they journeyed from the east, that they found a plain in the land of Shinar; and they dwelt there. And they said one to another, Go to, let us make brick, and burn them thoroughly. And they had brick for stone, and slime had they for morter. And they said, Go to, let us build us a city and a tower, whose top may reach unto heaven; and let us make us a name, lest we be scattered abroad upon the face of the whole earth. And the LORD came down to see the city and the tower, which the children of men builded. And the LORD said, Behold, the people is one, and they have all one language; and this they begin to do: and now nothing will be restrained from them, which they have imagined to do"* (Genesis 11:1-6). This work to reach God comes directly from Satan's nature as in he was the first to try to exalt himself as God.

    From the beginning of time, Satan has desired to elevate himself to be God. His evil nature is to exalt himself to be God. Before Satan was cast out of heaven, he was known as the "anointed cherub that covereth" In Ezekiel 28:14 it says, *"Thou art the anointed cherub that covereth; and I have set thee so: thou wast upon the holy mountain of God; thou hast walked up and down in the midst of the stones of fire. Thou wast perfect in thy ways from the day that thou wast created, till iniquity was found in thee. By the multitude of thy merchandise they have filled the midst of thee with violence, and thou hast sinned: therefore I will cast thee as profane out of the mountain of God: and I will destroy thee, O covering cherub, from the midst of the stones of fire. Thine heart was lifted up because of thy beauty, thou hast corrupted thy wisdom by reason of thy brightness: I will cast thee to the ground, I will lay thee before kings, that they may behold thee."* Satan was proud and wanted to be God. He was a high ranking angel and wants to be worshipped in any capacity. To not worship God is to worship Satan, no matter what you call your religion. Even if you perceive yourself as being God and are the master of your own destiny, you are still worshipping Satan.

  The God complex that Satan has is the same one he pours into man…The desire to be or be equal with the most high God. People become puffed up in themselves with the desire to be God or to tempt God and his authority. This mindset eliminates the need for a savior, so in essence man can save his own self. The very first temptation fed into man's nature to be like God. When Eve was in the garden, Satan approached her as a serpent and told her to eat of the "Tree of the Knowledge of Good and Evil." God had told Adam and Eve that they should not eat from that one particular tree or they would die. Satan lied to Eve and told her that she would not die, but would become as God knowing good and evil. Adam and Eve, desiring to have the knowledge left to God, ate from the tree, and the bible said that they immediately knew that they were naked. Satan from the beginning used deception and a play on words to deceive, just as he does today. He always dangles a carrot out that people perceive as good. God told them that they would die; Satan told them that they wouldn't die. Adam and Eve didn't immediately die in the flesh after they ate of the forbidden tree, but they immediately died spiritually and became cursed to return to the ground.

We have to remember our adversary knows religion, he knows worship; he knows the selfish desires that can be birthed out of men's hearts. He takes those desires and creates new belief structures. Some of the more known beliefs birthed out of the desire to be God are Hinduism, Buddhism, and New Age Thought.

Hinduism/ Buddhism

Hinduism is one of the world's major religions. According to a recent report there are over 1 billion Hindu believers in the world, with the vast majority of them coming from the nation of India. Hinduism has thousands of gods/devils that they worship. Of those thousands they have three that are the superior gods. Hindus believe that they have several reincarnated lives to get it right with god and when they have been good enough they become one with god. Everything is based upon outward works. The

THE JESUS EQUATION

more good you are the quicker you will become one with god. Hinduism just as many other religions has moral standards that it teaches and many embrace it because of the carnal good, but for eternal salvation it is clear that faith in Jesus Christ is essential to eternal life. Our adversary the devil, always twist details and creates these religions that have a form of goodness or godliness, but he always removes the key component. That component is Jesus. Hindus believe in heaven and hell. Hindus believe in moral goodness. Hindus worship a triune God, but the absolute necessity of Jesus is left out just as in many other religions.

    Demonically inspired beliefs will always have carrots of minor truths so that they may suck unsuspecting people into a snare, but when you look deep you can always find aspects of the flesh and worldliness within them. One of the largest marks of the work of the enemy within Hinduism is the caste system. I recently talked with a pastor in India and he spoke to me about how the "untouchables" are hungry for Jesus Christ. They have been discarded within Indian society according to their Hindu faith. The evangelizing of India for Jesus Christ is arising out of a discarded people. In Christianity Jesus came for the discarded, the poor, the beaten, and the suffering. The Hindu caste systems works directly against the purpose of Jesus. In India, the caste consists of five parts: the Brahmins (priests), the Kshatriyas (warriors and rulers), the Vaisyas (merchants), the Sudras (unskilled workers), and the Pariah (untouchables). Whichever caste you are born into, you are bound to stay there. These untouchables are "considered polluted and dirty, and do not rank as worthy humans in India. As discrimination is a part of their daily lives, Untouchables are shunned, insulted, banned from higher caste homes, made to eat and drink from separate utensils in public places, and are raped, burned, lynched, and gunned down." This mindset is formed out of Hinduism. The end result of all things demonic is destruction and death. It doesn't matter if there are some partially positive things that are associated with Hinduism. Many say that all religions have some truth in them, and they will lead you to God, but Jesus said, *"Then said Jesus unto them again, Verily, verily, I say unto you, I am the door of the sheep. All that ever came before me are thieves and robbers: but the sheep did not hear them. I am the door: by me if any man enter in, he shall be saved, and shall go in and out, and find pasture"* (John 10:7-9).

    Jesus gives life to the Christian faith; anything else is worthless and destitute. Jesus being the key equation in all things magnifies him as that target that must be removed. Jesus said that we must be of his sheepfold, a follower of him to inherit salvation. Buddhism which completely rejects the need for a God or savior indentifies the individual as his own savior, no heaven or hell, with an absolute goal of becoming enlightened. Some equate Buddhism as just a way of thinking, but its thoughts carry you far from anything relating to Jesus.

<u>Yoga</u>

    Hinduism is focused mainly in one part of the world, but its pagan influences are seen across the world, especially in American society. One of the greater ways Hinduism has affected Western society is through Yoga. Yoga is highly regarded as exercise that is extremely helpful to many ailments that people face. On the Hindu American Foundation website it says that Yoga is a "spiritual practice that is essential to the understanding and practice of Hinduism." It went on to discuss how westerners try to separate Yoga from it spiritual roots but it cannot be separated. The word "Yoga" within itself means to unite with the Hindu Gods. The positions that one takes while practicing Yoga are considered worship and takes participants into a place of oneness with Hindu gods. I have had many discussions with Christians in the United States on the spiritual dangers of practicing Yoga and many times it has fallen on deaf ears. Many Christian's who practice Yoga believe that it can be separated from its Hindu roots and many even start classes within their Christian churches. I am sure that there are many benefits to the natural body to practice Yoga, but we have to remember that the flesh will always lead us away from Christ.

New Age

   The more I watch television and movies, the more I see a new spiritual ideal arising; it focuses on humanity as a whole and unites God under one umbrella with many ways of reaching him. Some of your more well known celebrities have been promoting this newer religious mindset. One of the leading television talk show hosts that is known around the world advocates many paths to God. This all encompassing new age faith represents another of Satan's devices. As I have said many times, Satan doesn't care what you believe, as long as you lose

THE JESUS EQUATION

Jesus Christ. Satan doesn't have to get you hung up on one religion or one thought process, it is a mindset that opens people to everything spiritual and keeps people in a state of confusion, never really embracing anything.

A well known televangelist that saw his rise in 70's and 80's recently denounced most things Christian and started a new understanding of god. His new teachings are called, "The Gospel of Inclusion." This teaching says that there is no hell and God embraces all people no matter their belief or lifestyle. Many people who were on the fence about Jesus, because of their doubts and lifestyle, have openly indentified with this new teaching. This man and his teachings have been on major news outlets and some churches are starting to teach his doctrine. The thing that tricks a lot of new age adherents is that many do not deny the existence of Jesus and many of these new age cult beliefs incorporate Jesus in their teachings. They teach that Jesus was an enlightened teacher, and they put him on the same level as Muhammad, Buddha, and Gandhi. The thing I noticed about a lot of other religions is that they try to work in Jesus some kind of way in their teachings. They never present him as God or the door to our salvation, but they use him as an example. Demons many times will use Jesus as a draw, because of the power within the name. Paul the Apostle was contending with speaking of these deceptions when he said, *"But I fear, lest by any means, as the serpent beguiled Eve through his subtilty, so your minds should be corrupted from the simplicity that is in Christ. For if he that cometh preacheth another Jesus, whom we have not preached, or if ye receive another spirit, which ye have not received, or another gospel, which ye have not accepted, ye might well bear with him"* (2Corinthians 11:3-4). New Age religions teach "another Jesus", one that taught good morals and allowed men to be whoever they wanted to be. The Jesus I know said, *"Enter ye in at the strait gate: for wide is the gate, and broad is the way, that leadeth to destruction, and many there be which go in thereat: Because strait is the gate, and narrow is the way, which leadeth unto life, and few there be that find it"* (Matthew 7:13-14). The straight gate is accessing salvation through Jesus Christ and his word. The bible is clear that many false Christs will arise and deceive many. This rising of false Christs is in both our understanding and in people that proclaim they are the chosen for God's new way. If often amazes me how Satan can deceive people with things that are outwardly backwards.

    I have been following reports about a man that calls himself Jesus Christ and the anti-Christ at the same time. He wears a 666 tattoo on himself and teaches his followers to wear this tattoo. He has hundreds of radio broadcasts all around the world with a following in the hundreds of thousands. He proclaims the same spirit that was in Adam is the same spirit that is the one that was called the "anointed cherub that covereth" and that spirit is in him also. He says that God is behind everything and Satan doesn't exist. We know through studying scripture Satan is the one who was called the anointed cherub, and he was cast from heaven for trying to exalt himself as God. It is obvious that this man is under the power of demonic spirits. One might ask "are there that many people in the world that will believe such deception?" My answer is apparently so. Doctrines of devils always have an allure about them that anyone who is not strongly grounded in Jesus Christ will be sucked in. Many times Satan will go after people that are not strong minded, knowing that they will give in.

A while ago I was speaking to this gentleman and he started complaining about this organization and how it had destroyed his sister, and how her head was all messed up. He went on to tell me how he had escaped this group, but they seemed to keep finding him and harassing him, sending him letters and calling him. Oddly enough, a month or so after that I ran into another who needed prayer. He had escaped a cult and they were so entrenched into his life that he was fearful. I watched a video recently about an organization that follows and harasses people that speak against or try to leave the organization. They call their targets phones repeatedly, show up at their homes, and file lawsuits against them. Satan is serious about putting people in bondage. Once he has you in his grips he doesn't want to let go and he doesn't want you to embrace the true and living Jesus Christ either. When you are not in spiritual covenant with Jesus Christ, Satan has the authority to take you into bondage.

"*And that they may recover themselves out of the snare of the devil, who are taken captive by him at his will*" (2 Timothy 2:26). The message of this chapter of Timothy is instructing Christian ministers to teach individuals so that once they are Christ's they may get free of demonic oppression. Not only does Jesus Christ bring salvation, he brings spiritual liberty in this world and gives us authority over devils. This

THE JESUS EQUATION

liberty often competes with the excess of the world and the illusion of false teachings. New Age teachings are very dangerous and lead to a confused and lost soul. Jesus Christ has to be the center of all things and everything else must be discarded.

Chapter 5
Dividing the Brethren

"Wherefore she said unto Abraham, Cast out this bondwoman and her son: for the son of this bondwoman shall not be heir with my son, even with Isaac. And the thing was very grievous in Abraham's sight because of his son. And God said unto Abraham, Let it not be grievous in thy sight because of the lad, and because of thy bondwoman; in all that Sarah hath said unto thee, hearken unto her voice; for in Isaac shall thy seed be called" (Genesis 21:10-12).

So Much Division

Every day that I turn to the news, I see conflict in the Middle East. There seems to always be attacks going on or a threat of an attack against or by Israel. Most countries in the Middle East region of the world despise the nation of Israel. We have seen many military conflicts over territory during the history of the world, but the conflict within the scope of the area that the nation of Israel occupies is extremely intense. It is not only intense in this day and time but it was just as conflicted in biblical times. How could a land that is an eighth the size of the state of Florida, be so valuable and desired by so many. The answer is simple. 56% of the world's population regards this tiny plot of land as the birthplace of their religion. While only roughly seven million people live in this area, many billion people consider this holy land. Out of this region three religions were birthed: Judaism, Islam, and Christianity. Everyone believes their religion is the right way and everybody else's is wrong. The most interesting part of these three religions is not that they came from the same region, but also from the seed of one man named Abraham.

Seed of Abraham

Abraham is embraced by Judaism, Islam, and Christianity as the natural father for their faith. His lineage is said to be blessed by God. *"Seeing that Abraham shall surely become a great and mighty nation, and all the nations of the earth shall be blessed in him?"* (Genesis 18:18) God was so impressed with Abraham's faithfulness that he chose him to birth a nation of people into the world. When God approached Abraham about using him to produce a nation for him, he thought God to be jesting, because he and his wife were very old in age, and his wife was considered baron. Abraham's wife thought that maybe God wanted to use someone else to produce a child for Abraham so she suggested that Abraham have a child with his younger handmaiden Hagar the Egyptian. Abraham went along with it and had his first child, Ishmael. Abraham didn't realize the affliction he was bringing, because he thought it was God's will that he would have a son and so he made it happen through his own understanding of what God said.

When God gives us instruction, we should keep our belief in line with that of a little child. Children don't question, they just believe, even if it seems impossible. This seemingly impossible feat for God to give Abraham and Sarah a baby caused them to doubt. Satan many times speaks to us in logic and carnal understanding, that we may lose faith and attempt to control the outcome of situations. This taking control by our own understanding, many times leads to bondage. The moment that Ishmael was born, God pronounced the fruit of his life, *"And he will be a wild man; his hand will be against every man, and every man's hand against him; and he shall dwell in the presence of all his brethren"* (Genesis 16:12). Abraham's disobedience produced a child of disobedience.

As the years went by, God returned to Abraham and told him that he and his wife would have a child and he would be a blessing to all nations. Soon after, Abraham and his wife conceived a child. His name would be called Isaac. This child is the one that God ordained to bless all nations. After Isaac was born Ishmael began to mock the child. Sarah, the mother of Isaac heard the mocking and told Abraham to throw Hagar and Ishmael out of the house. After consulting God, Abraham threw them out. This is the first division within the house of Abraham. Ishmael grew up to start many tribes who modern day Arabs consider themselves to be descendants of.

Islam

Around 610 AD, Muhammad, who was an Arab, had a visitation by who he said was the angel Gabriel. Muhammad said that this angel had grabbed him and told him to recite the words he said. Muhammad thought to himself that he was possessed by devils as this angel kept hugging him and saying that he was Gabriel and that Muhammad was the messenger of God. As time went on Muhammad continued to have these visions and revelations. At one point he said that he was taken to the throne room of God, so close to God, that even Gabriel could not go for the sake of his wings being burned. He says that he met the other prophets before him, Jesus and Moses. The main revelation that was given to Muhammad was that he was the final prophet for the world, who was going to bring God's final instructions to the world.

When I read the story of Muhammad, I see the same "MO" or mode of operations for these deceiving spirits. Many times deceiving spirits have shown up to say, *"I am a great angel, you are a chosen prophet, and write down what I say"* and each and every time these spirits go on to dilute and destroy the foundation of Jesus Christ; such as the case in Islam. This angel placed Muhammad on the same level of Jesus, thereby nullifying the need for Jesus. Instead of acknowledging Jesus as the door to God, Muslims give honor to Muhammad.

With Satan it is always a diversion. It is

much easier to take some of a belief than all of a belief from someone, so Satan takes the attention away from Jesus and directs it to somewhere else allowing every other belief to stay intact. This is the reason you see parts and pieces of Christianity in other religions, but not the absolute of Jesus being the door, because Jesus being the door is the main component that makes Christianity what it is. Other religions promote love, self denial, and worldly restraint, drawing respect and admiration from the hearts of men. Islam, in its core moral values is seem very similar to Christianity, because it has a religious compass that makes sense to one that is looking to be good. Being good in a natural since though is not sufficient to God. Satan would have you to think that as long as you operate in good moral character that you are ok with God, no matter what you believe. Islam twist's even the morality of what is morally good by providing for the justification of carnal fighting against non-believers while Christianity says to love even enemies. Quran (48:29) - *"Muhammad is the messenger of Allah. And those with him are hard (ruthless) against the disbelievers and merciful among themselves"* While Christianity emphasizes i surrendering the flesh, but fighting in the spirit realm, Islam teaches to fight in the flesh. Quran (5:33) - *"The punishment of those who wage war against Allah and His messenger and strive to make mischief in the land is only this, that they should be murdered or crucified or their hands and their feet should be cut off on opposite sides or they should be imprisoned; this shall be as a disgrace for them in this world, and in the hereafter they shall have a grievous chastisement."*

THE JESUS EQUATION

As we view the fruits of Muhammad's labor within the religion of Islam, we see a religion that has over a billion followers worldwide. This one man and his embracing of a demonic spirit has affected billions of people. They have all denied the deity of Jesus and embraced an imposter. This imposter oppresses Christians all around the world. Satan would have you produce bondage in the lives of men through your disobedience. I am sure that Abraham never thought that this spirit of bondage would pass down and oppress many parts of the world.

I subscribe to a online journal that watches Christian issues around the world and I constantly get reports of Christian's being attacked and their churches burned down by the followers of Islam. When I take a view of Islam, Some of its leaders profess peace, but many of its adherents operate in violence. This is because Islam is birthed by the demonic and its fruit is unrighteousness. Jesus said that you shall know them by their fruits. Ishmael was born of a fleshly concern to conceive a child, and Isaac was conceived in the spirit because it was by faith. Islam births "wild men", just as God had pronounced that Ishmael would be a wild man. These wild men embrace the religious teachings that say to attack all those who do not accept Allah and his messenger Muhammad.

<u>Judaism</u>

Just as Ishmael mocked Isaac when he was born, the Jews have become the great enemy of many Muslims. Jews and Arabs were not able to live together from the start because one was the child of promise and the other was the child of bondage. *"For it is written, that Abraham had two sons, the one by a bondmaid, the other by a freewoman. But he who was of the bondwoman was born after the flesh; but he of the freewoman was by promise"* (Galatians 4:22-23). Judaism was birthed out of the desire for God to have a people. These people were called the Jews. From the lineage of Isaac came Jacob. Jacob birthed out the twelve tribes of Israel. Parts of these twelve tribes form what we know of the nation of Israel today. Though Israel started off as a nation that was accepted in God's eyes, they have now completely rejected God and have embraced another spirit.

      Judaism, at its inception, embraced all that is Christian, but just like all the other faiths, they redirected themselves when they decided to deny Jesus being the son of God. We can find the meat of the Jewish faith within the scriptures of the Holy Bible. It is commonly referred to as the Old Testament. Their understandings of God can be summarized mainly within the first five books of the Old Testament called the Torah. When God first anointed Israel to be a chosen nation, he established a covenant with them. This covenant consisted of the promises of God for them and the 613 laws that the nation of Israel was instructed to follow.

  From the start of God's relationship with Israel they were constantly angry and complained against God. This bad attitude brought many problems for Israel. When the problems persisted, many resolved themselves to other god's and started to create their own understandings of God against scriptures. These false understandings were formed under the guise of an oral law which became passed down through several generations. When Jesus had arrived on earth and presented himself to the Jews as their savior, the keepers of this oral law or commonly known as *"the Pharisees and Sadducees"*, became his largest adversary. Jesus is commonly found rebuking them in scriptures, *"But woe unto you, scribes and Pharisees, hypocrites! for ye shut up the kingdom of heaven against men: for ye neither go in yourselves, neither suffer ye them that are entering to go in"* (Matthew 23:13).   Even though the Jews were the chosen ones and Jesus came according to prophecy, they still rejected him. Even though Jesus did many signs and wonders among the people, they still rejected him. All the prophets that had come before where received and counted holy but when the true and living messiah came; they couldn't receive it. Satan will always try to take a good work and twist and turn it to a point that is no good in God's eyes anymore.

   Satan had taken hold of the minds of the religious leaders. Satan allowed them to hold on to all that was not Jesus, because he knew that the rejection of him in itself was sufficient to bring spiritual death to them. Satan threw every piece of deception he could muster at Jesus....he tempted him in the wilderness, he betrayed him through one of his disciples, Jesus was rejected by his sheep, they wrote off Jesus as a sorcerer. When you deeply research the scriptures Jesus came in such a humble and lowly manner, the prideful leaders would not accept him. He was someone who was not of their class or stature and he was not of the Levite priesthood lineage. These religious leaders were looking for a little more fleshly greatness. Satan always appeals to the flesh and if

THE JESUS EQUATION

he can use your flesh to get you to reject God he will do it. Christians have to be careful that they do not allow mistakes and lack of faith to bring division and bondage to others.

Chapter 6
Angel of Light

"For such are false apostles, deceitful workers, transforming themselves into the apostles of Christ. And no marvel; for Satan himself is transformed into an angel of light" (2Co 11:13).

<u>Deception in the Church</u>

Many years ago my mother gave me a book called "The Century of the Holy Spirit". It chronicled the last hundred years of the Pentecostal and Charismatic Renewal starting with the Azusa Street revival in the early nineteen hundreds. Out of this movement, thousands of denominations where birthed that called themselves "spirit filled or prophetic." When I look at the church today there are tens of thousands of denominations. Some estimates have said there are over 40 thousand different denominations across the world. This number is staggering considering there is only one church that Jesus Christ leads. When I drive down the street in Georgia there seems to be a church on every corner and everyone claims to have the proper way to worship God. Reality sunk in when I pulled into a strip mall parking lot and realized that of the four business spaces there were four churches huddled together, each with their own sign, their own door, and pastor. Many times churches do not fellowship with other churches because of differences of beliefs. I ask myself how can there be 40,000 different ways to believe in Jesus? How can there be 40,000 different ways to worship the most high God. Just one church in his word, but 40,000 that do not associate many times with each other. Why so much division and disagreement. Is man just that picky?

    As much as many would like to ignore or pretend like it doesn't exist, Satan and his army have been waging a war against the church since it was first established. This war has ultimately been one of dividing and conquering. This "divide and conquer" strategy is as old as time and the enemy knows that if he can keep the people of God in disagreement then he can destroy them piece by piece. Jesus said, *"And if a kingdom be divided against itself, that kingdom cannot stand. And if a house be divided against itself, that house cannot stand"* (Mark 3:24-25). Some might say "well even though the physical church is not together the spiritual church is one." Yes, the true church is united in the spirit, but the question becomes which physical churches are attached to the spirit of God. If I go to any one of these denominations they will surely tell you the spirit of God is with their church, but sadly the truth is that some, if not many are mistaken.

    When a church is mistaken about their

spiritual guidance or direction, error enters quickly. Sometimes a "spiritual revelation" will come to a person and if it puts them in disagreement with the organization or Christian body they are in association with, they separate from them and either find a Christian body that agrees with their "revelation" or they start their own. If the spirit of God really gave them revelation then they are right for their decision, but the problem comes when it is not the spirit of God. There is most certainly a counterfeit holy spirit, a counterfeit Jesus, and a counterfeit church. These work to undermine the work of Jesus Christ in the body. We understand by scripture that Jesus Christ is the head of the church. He loved the church so much that he gave his life for it. He is the high priest forever and eternally sits on the right hand of God. Satan would love so much to have people worshiping him instead of Christ and think that they are doing right.

    No one receives a counterfeit knowingly. It is always by deception. This substitute image serves to remove the one person that can give us eternal life. His name is Jesus. The Bible says, *"Now the Spirit speaketh expressly, that in the latter times some shall depart from the faith, giving heed to seducing spirits, and doctrines of devils;"* (1Timothy 4:1). Devils create churches and evil beliefs and give them to men as revelation. Men are seduced into thinking they have something special that wasn't revealed until now and they are the chosen one to reveal it. Sometimes revelations are completely against God's written word, but as usual, justification is given for the conflicting words. Many people these days are searching for a new word and a new revelation. Some want to be the latest and greatest and others want to stay in social agreement with the world's standards. Satan specializes in giving words, he started off with a "new word and revelation" in genesis with Adam and Eve, telling them that they would be like gods knowing good and evil and they would not die. Every soul that has entered this life has suffered a curse for Adam and Eve's transgression. Jesus came that we might have an exit from this curse.

False Revivals

    Several years ago I was riding in the car with a co-worker and he told me about this great revival that was going on in Florida. He told me that this great revivalist and healer had come to Georgia and he was going to be operating in signs and miracles here also. I didn't attend the event but I looked up the minister that rose to prominence with all these signs and wonders couple of years ago. He claimed to be establishing a new powerful revival. Thousands upon thousands flocked to his services and there were many claims of healings and deliverance every day of the week. Many of the services emphasized outward strange manifestations and violent healings that appeared to be heavily mocking the things of God. This minister spoke in his services of an angel that had appeared to him and told him he was to establish this new work. He said the angel told him his name was "Emma" and told him to tell the people its name. As I listened to this man preach he said that we all know that name of Jesus, but we need to now know the name of the angel Emma, and the angel will do great miracles. Watching videos of him and discerning the demonic involved I noticed a tattoo on his arm. It was Japanese writing and it was surrounded in yellow. When I looked up Japanese deities, I found there was one called Emma-o. This Emma-o deity resided in the yellow springs under the earth as the God of the underworld. Just as so many times before evil spirits show up in people's lives, tell them they have a new revelation and proceed to try and remove Jesus Christ out of his position of authority and power. The devil has used this trick over and over again to gain the trust of non-discerning Christians and have them turn from Christ to another messenger.

   Satan is called the accuser of the brethren, because he lies constantly seeking to spin and stir offense among the righteous. He sows discord mixed with false understanding and then appeals to the prideful heart. In these last days the visible church is certainly at its weakest point, allowing all types of strange beliefs into the church, outwardly calling good evil and evil good.

<u>Jehovah's Witness</u>

      One Sunday morning I was getting ready to go to church and I noticed some people walking down the sidewalk in the front of my house. These people were dressed up nicely and were going door to door. When they came to my door I answered it with an interest because I wanted to see what they were talking about. They immediately presented themselves as Christians and wanted to give me some readings that were distributed through their organization. I refused the info but then they asked me a question. They said, "Do you know the name of God?" I replied with a resounding yes and named a few of the names he was known by in bible scripture. At that point they informed me that God only has one name, "Jehovah", and if we are going to have a good relationship with him we have to know and embrace this name.

    I remembered a few months prior when I had sent out a email newsletter for my ministry and someone in the email list replied to it and asked me if knew the name of God. I kept replying with different biblical names, including Jehovah, but he insisted on focusing on this one name. There is a reason why the Jehovah's Witnesses call themselves this name. The majority of their faith is wrapped around the name "Jehovah."

    At this point of speaking with the people, I started to inquire more of their insistence of focusing on the name "Jehovah." Immediately the man with the group started to rattle off these sayings that he considered wise and he said he was quoting Gandhi. I was a little taken back that he would reference at spiritual leader of another religion in relation to Christianity. I told him it was foolishness to think that he could justify quoting someone who was unrighteous to add creditability to his statement. As the conversation went deeper I asked him if he had the Holy Spirit. He told me no. I asked him if he knew any of the gifts of the Holy Spirit. He didn't know what I was talking about. It was very apparent that I was speaking to someone who was under the power of another spirit that was not of God. Later, as I began to research this religion, I found fundamental twists in teachings that served the devices of Satan. Although the Jehovah Witnesses may on the surface appear to be safe. It is a very dangerous religion.

THE JESUS EQUATION

The Jehovah's Witnesses believe that Jesus Christ returned in the spirit in 1914 to establish his kingdom on earth. They forgot the scripture that says, *"Behold, he cometh with clouds; and every eye shall see him, and they also which pierced him: and all kindreds of the earth shall wail because of him. Even so, Amen"* (Revelations 1:7). When Jesus Christ returns he will come powerfully, not secretly. Satan likes to form new religions that are similar to Christianity and twist them up with lies. He makes subtle twists in scripture and understanding that undermines the basis for the gospel. With the Jehovah's Witnesses Satan needed to move Jesus out of the way to make room for focus on the name, "Jehovah." If people believe Jesus Christ has already returned it dilutes their understanding and relationship with him. Satan wants people to not focus on Jesus. He wants to remove that aspect from our life. When Jesus Christ is not the center of our life, we lose all benefit of God. Jesus Christ said that he is the door and the only access to God. Jesus even said that anyone trying to reach God by any other way is a thief and a robber (John 10:1). Jehovah's Witnesses do not equate Jesus to being God. They see him as an angel of God.

    One of the most obvious tactics that Satan has taken with the Jehovah's Witnesses is that they do not believe Jesus rose in the flesh but in the spirit. Even though when they found the rock rolled away from the tomb the body of Jesus was gone. Even though he appeared to many and even allowed the disciples to touch his wounds, the Jehovah's Witnesses deny this. The reason it is denied is that Jesus' authority and power must be diluted. His work on the cross, his overcoming Satan, and his bodily resurrection, speaks to who Jesus is to us. It is through him we are able to overcome this world, it is through him we can walk in authority; it is through him that we will overcome death. Jehovah's Witness marginalize Jesus and deny the indwelling of the Holy Spirit. By rejecting Jesus, they also reject the Holy Spirit. This is why the gentlemen I was speaking to said that he did not have the Holy Spirit. The Jehovah's Witness beliefs remove Christ and deny a bodily temple for the Holy Spirit. Jesus Christ is the door and the Holy Spirit is the power. All represent a person of God, but with different operations. In my studies I read an article that one of Jehovah Witness leaders wrote and they tried to justify why they didn't believe in the three persons of God. They tried to use reason and logic to say their God wasn't "three headed and freakish." This statement goes to the mindset of Jehovah's Witness and them trying to rationalize and equate God to a more understandable nature. That's why they say:

    1. Jesus came back in the spirit because (he is invisible and now his return is rationalized)

    2. Jesus rose as a spirit out of the grave (its sound more rational that actually making the flesh alive again)

    3. The Holy Spirit is a force and not a person (takes away the question of who is the spirit)

4. Dead cease to exist (forces believers hope to all received on this earth)

Even the belief that Jesus came already to establish his millennial reign in 1914 satisfies the rational and allows men of corrupt minds to regulate God on this planet. We have to be careful of doctrines of devils twisting and diluting the word of God for their gain. The Jehovah's Witness want to establish a carnal kingdom on this earth with the invisible Jesus as the head. If Satan can keep all of our hope and aspirations in this world, we will surely perish.

Mormons

When I reflect on the Mormons, I cannot help but think of spiritual wickedness in high places. As I did my research on the Mormons, I realized that their beliefs were nowhere near to being Christian, and no matter what anyone says this religion is demonic from the bottom to the top.
As I was growing up I looked at the Mormons as being just another Christian denomination and when I would see the TV ads on the Church of Latter Day Saints, I would think that it was good they were spreading the message of the Gospel of Jesus. Even when you view some of their sermon promos online, you would certainly be convinced of their belief in the same Jesus of Nazareth that came in the flesh, died, and rose from the grave. There is no doubt the Mormons believe in another Jesus. This is the same problem that the Apostle Paul contended with in his day... *"But I fear, lest by any means, as the serpent beguiled Eve through his subtilty, so your*

THE JESUS EQUATION

minds should be corrupted from the simplicity that is in Christ. For if he that cometh preacheth another Jesus, whom we have not preached, or if ye receive another spirit, which ye have not received, or another gospel, which ye have not accepted, ye might well bear with him" (2 Corinthians 11:3-4).

It is by subtle twists and turns in doctrine that turn into wide holes that swallow generations of souls. Satan from the beginning has sought to remix God's directions to leave people lost. Every generation multiple false prophets rise and profess things that God has not said. These unsuspecting men and women embrace devils usually out of their own inadequacies...the need to be special or fulfill a carnal lust.

The Mormon faith was founded by Joseph Smith. His trade before becoming prophet was being a treasure hunter. His story of being chosen by a special angel is very similar to other false prophets. He claims that he was visited by an angel named Moroni. This angel informed him that he was God's chosen to bring truth to people. He claims that he was given golden plates and these plates had special instructions on them. The Story only gets deeper and odd from there.

Mormons believe that God lives on a planet called Kolob. They believe that God has a wife and they produce spirit babies. When we die, if we have done well in this life they believe that we will become Gods and Goddesses. As far as symbols are concerned, many of the symbols on their temples are Masonic in origin. Joseph Smith was a mason before he founded the Mormon Church. A lot of the rituals and symbols of the Mormon Church are identical to

THE JESUS EQUATION

Masonic symbols. Mormons deny that the blood of Jesus is sufficient for sins.

In one of the holy books of Mormon's it states that black people's skin is a curse that God put on them for being disobedient. Book of Mormon (2 Nephi 5:21) - *"And he had caused the cursing to come upon them, yea, even a sore cursing, because of their iniquity. For behold, they had hardened their hearts against him, that they had become like unto a flint; wherefore, as they were white, and exceedingly fair and delightsome, that they might not be enticing unto my people the Lord God did cause a skin of blackness to come upon them."*

When I read the Mormon texts, my discernment says that the religion was written in the flesh. A demon inspired Joseph Smith and left him to his fleshly writings. In one part of the story he claims that John the Baptist appeared to him and made him apart of the Levitical priesthood. Then he says that Peter, John, and James of the Bible appeared to him and made him apart of the the Melchesdik priesthood. As I read more on Mormons I found my head spinning as if it was written by a confused mind. It was obvious that this religion was formed to confuse and bind minds.

Satan loves to mix in confusion and bad doctrine around so that people will not know what to believe. He tries to elevate angels and new prophets to eliminate the power of Jesus. If you look into most new revelations that are adverse to the teachings of the bible, most of the time there is an angel and/or a prophet that is chosen to bring new knowledge. Jesus spoke of these deceptions that were to come when he said, "And many false prophets shall rise, and shall deceive many" (Matthew 24:11). Within the Mormon Church itself there are over 14 million members. This is why it is so important for Christians to fight against and resist false doctrine/revelation from entering into the church. One bad revelation or one false word can lead millions astray.

<u>Mammon</u>

I had visited a local church for a while after I had rededicated my life to Christ. I noticed they spoke a lot about money and attaining all these natural riches through Christ. As they read scriptures on attaining wealth, I not knowing what to think being a babe in Christ, started to study the subject of natural wealth attainment and God. I researched everything they said. I was not going to be drawn away like I was before. If God had a pot of Gold for me, I was going to find it at the end of the rainbow. If a lie had been given, it was going to be exposed. I never found that pot of gold, that Bentley, or mansion on the hill. What I found was that God's love was no more absent from the poor man on the street than the rich man on the hill…and those that do see the rich different than the poor, God calls them judges with evil thoughts (James 2:4). As a matter of fact wealth attainment has nothing to do with how close you are to God. Some preach that God's great men of faith get great wealth. I wonder how some cling to this obviously demonic teaching considering that the Bible states that, *"gain is not godliness"* (1 Timothy 6:5). And though this church had thousands of members who religiously opened their study bibles and listened intently from page to page, the church continued to flourish naturally in a message that was obviously not from God. How can a church with so many people who earnestly seek God be carried away with doctrine like this? I believe that the question is are they really seeking God or are they gathered for what their flesh wants to hear.

It is certain that the love of money is the root of all evil and this evil has invaded the Church, in its most diluted position. Satan's goal is ultimately to get you to lose your salvation. When you have a relationship with Jesus Christ he tries to unwind and replace your belief structure. He first weakens your position, introduces small twists of doctrine and belief, dilutes your spiritual discernment, then brings in the large error to completely disrupt and destroy your relationship with Jesus Christ. Scripture says in the last days people will gather themselves teachers who will teach them what they want to hear. I hear people talking about the Church staying relevant in today's society. Staying relevant is another way of saying, "I am going to dilute or change God's message to attract more people or keep the ones we have".

They might say *"Lets start a church. What do people want to hear? I know, lets tell them they can stay in sin and get rich. I am sure we will have a mega church in no time. God wants his people to be blessed and Jesus died for our sins and we don't have to worry about that"* You might say you can't imagine anyone saying that, but actions speak louder than words, *"Wherefore by their fruits ye shall know them"* (Matthew 7:20).

THE JESUS EQUATION

<u>Sensual</u>

The bible says that we as Christians are at war with the flesh. Even the Apostle Paul said that he had to overcome his flesh daily. It is certain that our own desires have a profound influence on our daily choices. Many great and honorable men and women have fallen to weaknesses in their mortal bodies. This point of access keeps us needing a continual relationship with Jesus Christ. He is the only one that can keep us from our own desires. If the devil can get someone to reject Christ or dilute the relationship with Christ, the persons own flesh will do the rest of the job in destroying hopes of salvation. Our relationship with Jesus Christ unleashes the power of the Holy Spirit to keep us from our sinful selves. When Christ came he combined soul and spirit so that now when we receive Jesus Christ as our lord and savior we become born again into the spirit. As Paul stated, our natural selves become quickened through the power of the Holy Spirit (Romans 8:11) and is able to keep us.

Although the Holy Spirit has been made available to believers to walk in authority, many have put this authority down to walk after the flesh. With so many giving in to the flesh, many write it off as the way of the world. When I first got married, a man that I knew told me that after I was married for a year it was okay to find a mistress. He spoke to me as someone who felt they were giving good advice. All he knew was that he couldn't contain himself and others he knew through life couldn't either. So the way of the world to this man was to have extra marital affairs. He believed that it was natural to have more than one woman. Satan's first attack on man was to make evil appear good and good appear evil. From the beginning God made marriage between one man and one woman and he blessed it. Any combination outside of this blessed order is defilement. God said that "marriage is honorable in all, the bed undefiled". God gave us marriage to keep a sacred union with him even during the satisfaction of our carnal selves. Satan doesn't want Christians to marry because he knows that if he can keep you in unrighteous relationships, it will keep separated from God. He wants to defile your bedroom. Defilement of "everything that God meant to be holy" is the game the enemy is playing. Marriage is so honorable in God's eyes that it is compared to Jesus Christ's relationship to the church. *"Therefore as the church is subject unto Christ, so let the wives be to their own husbands in every thing. Husbands, love your wives, even as Christ also loved the church, and gave himself for it; That he might sanctify and cleanse it with the washing of water by the word,"* (Ephesians 5:24-26) Marriage is a covenant relationship just as Christ made a covenant with the Church.

    Today we see men marrying men and women marrying women. Government and businesses are beginning to reject and punish organizations that stand for the Christian view of marriage. Openly gay ministers are being ordained in the church. I have asked myself many times how could a church that proclaims Jesus Christ ordain gay ministers. I now understand that spiritual discernment has been destroyed in parts of the church to the point where people cannot tell the difference between good and evil. People are letting their own struggles dictate what must be good. They say, "since I haven't been able to change then this must be how God made me" and "since God made me this way, he will accept me without change." *"For the time will come when they will not endure sound doctrine; but after their own lusts shall they heap to themselves teachers, having itching ears;" (2Timothy 4:3)*. Satan has exploited the lusts of men to the point that they will even ignore good spiritual teaching and seek those who will teach them what they want to hear to continue their sinful lifestyles. People are looking for answers that fit in their personal world and the devil is eager to give them an answer. I recently watched a broadcast by a major TV personality and they had guests on saying that homosexuality was a gift from God, and that everybody was going to heaven. This type of programming fits into the agenda to remove Christ and our need for a savior and replace it with sin.

    When I started my first church, I was so excited! I rented out a little warehouse building and started having service. It was just a few of us, but I was happy about what God was doing. A few months in, I was at the church one day and the maintenance man told me that a church was opening up in the next building over from ours. I being interested to meet my fellow brothers in Christ, went over to introduce myself. I spoke to the pastor and he told me they had 300 members and were growing at a rapid pace. Something didn't seem quite right about him so I looked up his church online. To my amazement, they were a openly gay congregation, including the pastor. I became conflicted in my soul. How could this openly gay pastor and his congregation, have so much success and excitement going on? The praise music would blast beyond the building and the cars would pack the parking lot all the time! I prayed to God about it and he said that you cannot judge the move of his spirit by numbers or natural attainment. Oh course I knew this, but I wanted to have numbers and a visibly prospering church! This is where the temptation comes in with a righteous man. Should he preach what is true and let the cards fall where they may or should the message change to appeal to more people. I thought about my grandmother and her little white church. She was so faithful, uncompromising, and committed for so many years yet she never saw more than a few attendees each week. Though she spent her days praying for people and visiting the sick, most never joined the work she was doing. The further you press into the things of God, the more you realize that the ultimate blessings of God, may never be seen by man and if you are seeking the affirmation of man, you most of the time find yourself outside the good graces of God.

      One day I had a dream that I was going to church; someone had suggested this particular church, so we went. The church was massive, I remember all the people that were headed into the building. It was a grand event. As we walked in the long line in the building we came to the opening of the sanctuary, I noticed that there was a casket with a dead body at the front of the pulpit in the church. I quickly looked over and I saw no one seated for service, I was in line to view a body. I was told that it was the preacher's son. As I looked in the coffin, I noticed the man's eyes were moving and all of a sudden his arms started flipping around. A thought came to my mind that "sometimes dead bodies still move, before the rigor sets in." As the thoughts raced through my head, the body started to flip around in the coffin, kind of like a fish out of water. All of the deacons jumped from the pulpit and were wrestling with this dead body. As I consulted God about this, it was revealed to me that there are ministers with massive congregations that are preaching in the flesh, and while they appear to be alive the living spirit of God has departed from them. I sought answers of why it was the preacher's son and it was revealed to me that this is a generational problem. I have thought about this dream many times and I know that Satan has worked to destroy the spirit of man and to remove any connection to Christ. He knows that if the head is removed, the body cannot stand. Satan looks to destroy the heads of churches and have them operating in the flesh so that the fruits of their labor will be unrighteousness. I thank God that Jesus Christ is the ultimate head of the church as a whole, and as long as we remain connected to him, we will always stand.

Chapter 7
Name Above All Names

"That at the name of Jesus every knee should bow, of things in heaven, and things in earth, and things under the earth; And that every tongue should confess that Jesus Christ is Lord, to the glory of God the Father" (Philippians 2:10-11).

<u>Our Salvation</u>

I know it was the blood. I know it was the blood. I know it was the blood for me. One day when I was lost he died up on the cross. I know it was the blood for me. *"And Jesus Christ who is the faithful witness, and the first begotten of the dead, and the prince of the kings of the earth. Unto him that loved us, and washed us from our sins in his own blood, and hath made us kings and priests unto God and his father; to him be glory and dominion forever and ever. Amen"* (Revelations 1:4-5). Jesus died on the cross and shed his blood for all people. He lost his life so that we may have access to salvation. By no other name can we be saved. Jesus is the door, the truth, the light. There is no other way. I emphasize Jesus, because he is the key to salvation. "I am the door: by me if any man enter in, he shall be saved, and shall go in and out, and find pasture" (John 10:9). Many don't realize that this was the plan all along. Revelations 13:8 states that the lamb, Jesus Christ, was slain since the foundation of the world. The evidence of the savior coming and the need for a savior is present throughout the scripture. From the beginning of the world when Abel offered the firstlings of his sheep and being counted righteous he was murdered; to the blood sacrifice of the animals at the altar of God as commanded by the Law of Moses. This insufficiency of man's sacrifices made evident the need of a savior. No amount of animal bloodshed was able to cover man's sin. It had to be the blood of Jesus. He was an innocent man, free from sin, the purest of them all, yet sentenced to death like a murderer.

    Jesus became a curse for us, "for it is written cursed is everyone that hangeth on a tree" (Galatians 3:13). Before Jesus if anyone sinned or if they did not follow all of the regulations of the law they were cursed. When Jesus was crucified on the cross he bore all of our sins and sickness. By this action he became a curse for a season. His bloodshed was the final sacrifice for sin. This victory gave us access to God, without regulations, without special priests, or temple sacrifices, etc. Jesus became the eternal high priest and we as followers became kings and priests. The blood of Jesus is so powerful that demons run at the name of it. It flows in like a tsunami to a repentant heart and cleans perfectly. What else can make God forget we were a sinful, unworthy people? The blood of Jesus is the pardon that the prisoners of sin need. The blood of Jesus is like the 11:59 call from the governor that took the walking dead off the executioners table. Demons know that when the blood flows, their fight is over. It is the evidence of Christ's victory over Satan. Even though we fight Satan constantly; he has already been defeated. He is already on a one way ticket to hell; he just wants to take as many people with him as possible. We must choose between heaven or hell, life or death, spirit or flesh. The blood is available to redeem, yet we must accept it for it to accept us. To choose the blood is to turn our backs on sin and worship God in Spirit and truth.

  When a woman gives birth to a child, her water breaks; and then as the child comes the blood flows. As Jesus died on the cross, he released water and blood (John 19:34-35), signifying the birth of a new season. It ushered in a season of true justification before God, salvation by grace, and an adoption as children of God. As the new life sprang from the woman as she gave birth, in our repentant heart we spring forth as new children. So no longer are we servants but sons of the most high God. Galatians 4:7. Children of God, be blessed and hold on to that which is good. Love your neighbor as yourself because without love we are nothing.

  You are no longer servants in bondage, but free in Jesus Christ. And remember there is no compromise in God. The sinful, whether on the street or in the pulpit, will be judged and cast into the lake of fire. Repent! *"many will say to me in that day, Lord, Lord, have wenot prophesied in thy name? and in thy name have cast out devils? And in thy name done many wonderful works? And then will I profess unto them, I never you: depart from me, ye that work iniquity"* (Matt 7:23).

Secure In Jesus

Christians can rest assured that there is no other name or any other way that we can attain eternal life. If Christ is the door, then you have to go through him to get to anything associated with God. God said in the Bible, to accept Jesus Christ is to accept him and to deny Jesus Christ is to deny him. This is what makes Jesus the key to all things. This is why Satan wants to remove Jesus.

Any other God, any other belief, or any other pathway leads to destruction. When we look in Revelation 13:8 it says that the Lamb of God was slain from the foundation of the world. Most have read about his 33 year walk on earth in the flesh, we know he died in the flesh, and overcame death to rule and reign with God, but his birth in Bethlehem was not the start of his days just like the cross of Calvary was not the end. All things manifested in this world are first birthed in the spirit. Jesus was always slain, he had always shed his blood for us, He was always positioned to welcome all to his kingdom that would believe. Satan would have you limit and rationalize Jesus to earthly standards so that anything outside of a carnal nature would not fit. Jesus will not fit into carnal understanding. The very power to call him lord is by the Holy Spirit. In 1 Corinthians 12:3 it says *"Wherefore I give you to understand, that no man speaking by the Spirit of God calleth Jesus accursed:*

THE JESUS EQUATION

and that no man can say that Jesus is the Lord, but by the Holy Ghost." It is in spiritual power that Christ comes into our life and it is by that power that we are saved.

Many may believe in the man, Jesus, but the belief in the power behind Jesus tends to be absent. As I read the Old Testament, the manifestation of Jesus Christ kept showing up time and time again. When we read the story of Shadrach, Meshach, and Abednego we see that they were thrown into a fiery furnace for their refusal to bow down to anyone outside of our lord Jehovah. There were two amazing things about this story. The first is that these men through the power of God were able to escape death and the second is that there was a fourth person that showed up in the flames. When we look in Daniel 3:25 it says *"He answered and said, Lo, I see four men loose, walking in the midst of the fire, and they have no hurt; and the form of the fourth is like the Son of God."* Jesus Christ our lord and savior was even saving people before he came into the flesh.... THAT IS POWER! This is why Satan would have you to deny Christ, cause Jesus Christ is able to save you no matter where you are, no matter if it seems that there is no hope he is there. Our carnal minds tell us that if God doesn't save us before we get entangled by our situations that there is no hope. Even as Jesus walked the earth, some would mock him when a person would die, before he was able to reach him, but even the finality of death could not contain the power of Jesus.

When Lazarus had been buried for four days, Jesus went to the grave and resurrected him. It didn't matter that decay had started, and he was in his burial tomb. In the darkest of darkest times, Jesus is the answer. When Jesus Christ had died on the cross, he became a curse (Galatians 3:13) and went to hell to preach the "spirits in prison" (1 Peter 3:19). Without Jesus Christ, there was no Salvation for the lost. His conquering of death established him as the key to all in heaven and on earth. Jesus Christ's position as authority and answer to all makes him enemy number one to all things evil. Devils cannot destroy or undo anything that Jesus has done or will do, but they can trick us as humans into missing out on the greatest blessing to be presented to the earth.

  Jesus will come, he will judge the quick and the dead, Satan and his angels will endure eternal torment, Jesus will reign over heaven and earth, he will stand forever in glory...These things are certain and Satan knows that. What is not certain is who will reign with Jesus. All humans have a choice between life and death. Our closeness with Christ is attained through our denial of this world. Denying of false religion/doctrine and the denial of the desires of the flesh are must haves to walk with Jesus Christ. *"Then spake Jesus again unto them, saying, I am the light of the world: he that followeth me shall not walk in darkness, but shall have the light of life"* (John 8:12). Jesus is our light and when we receive him we walk in the light, when we deny him we remain in darkness. Jesus is the Equation for all things blessed and eternal.

THE JESUS EQUATION

"I am the living bread which came down from heaven: if any man eat of this bread, he shall live for ever: and the bread that I will give is my flesh, which I will give for the life of the world" (John 6:51).

THE JESUS EQUATION

www.ingramcontent.com/pod-product-compliance
Lightning Source LLC
Chambersburg PA
CBHW051700040426
42446CB00009B/1234